Ekaterinoslav: One Family's Journey to America

"Jane Yolen, master storyteller of myth and fantasy offers us a different kind of tale this time—a compelling, unsentimental family narrative told eloquently in verse. She recreates 'a lifetime, a country, a shtetl' and one family's circuitous and rocky journey toward the American Dream. In her vivid, poetic resurrection of family, Jane Yolen confirms what I always suspected—that storytelling is an integral part of her ancestral DNA."

—MIRA BARTOK, author of *The Memory Palace* (New York Times bestselling memoir, National Book Critics Circle Award Winner)

"Jane Yolen's new work, *Ekaterinoslav*, is a moving memoir, part family story, part immigrant fable. The strong narrative pull of the poems propels the reader forward wanting to know what will happen next with each personality deftly captured in the sparest descriptions of a few sharp lines. The shifting mood of the story weaves gracefully through the poems, skillfully translating historical facts and family truths. The final poem offers a personal, powerful conclusion, as Yolen moves from the past to the present using poetry 'to reinvent moment and memory.'"

—SYLVIA M. VARDELL, Ph.D., author of *Poetry Aloud Here* and *The Poetry Teacher's Book of Lists*

Things to Say to a Dead Man: Poems at the End of a Marriage and After

"*Things to Say to a Dead Man* is a stunning book. What Jane Yolen offers the reader is nothing but the truth: this is what grief looks like, sounds like, smells, like, feels like. Only one who has loved so deeply can mourn this profoundly. *Things to Say to a Dead Man* does what all good poetry should do: it wakes the reader up, reminding us that life is fleeting and therefore full of sadness and therefore utterly beautiful."

—LESLÉA NEWMAN, Poet Laureate of Northampton, MA 2008-2010, author of *Nobody's Mother*

"Written in the final months of her husband's battle with cancer and during the five years after his death, Jane Yolen's *Things to Say to a Dead Man* is a quiet and elegant chronicle of grief."

—*Minneapolis Star Tribune*

"Common language, clarity, and precision distinguish these poems. As long as there are grievers, these poems will have a grateful readership."

T0094648

HOLY COW! PRESS BOOKS BY JANE YOLEN:

Ekaterinoslav: One Family's Passage to America,
A Memoir in Verse

(2012)

Things to Say to a Dead Man:
Poems at the End of a Marriage and After

(2011)

THE
BLOODY
TIDE

POEMS
ABOUT POLITICS
AND POWER

JANE YOLEN

HOLY COW! PRESS :: DULUTH, MINNESOTA :: 2014

The Bloody Tide: Poems about Politics and Power © 2014 by Jane Yolen.
Author photograph by Jason Stemple.

Painting on the cover:
The Garden of Earthly Delights, Hell panel (detail) by Hieronymus Bosch.

Book and cover design by Anton Khodakovsky.

First printing, 2014

ISBN 9978-0-9859818-3-9

10 9 8 7 6 5 4 3 2 1

This project is supported in part by grant awards from the Ben and Jeanne Overman Charitable Trust, the Elmer L. and Eleanor J. Andersen Foundation, the Cy and Paula DeCosse Fund of the Minneapolis Foundation, The Lenfestey Family Foundation, and by gifts from individual donors.

Holy Cow! Press books are distributed to the trade by Consortium Book Sales & Distribution, c/o Perseus Distribution, 210 American Drive, Jackson, TN 38301.

For inquiries, please write to: Holy Cow! Press, Post Office Box 3170, Mount Royal Station, Duluth, MN 55803.

Visit *www.holycowpress.org*

Acknowledgements

Listening to the News Reminds Me of Yeats © 2012, *Conclave Magazine*

Breathing Water © 2011 *Pirene's Fountain, Japan Anthology; Issue 4*

The Recycled Orchestra © 2013 *AuthorsforEarthDay blog*

Fahrenheit © 2013, *Sister Fox's Field Guide to Writing*

Impedimenta © 2001, *Peregrine: A Journal*

The Importance of a Single Word © 2009, *Pirene's Fountain*

The Rivers of Babylon: In Memoriam © 1960, *Chicago Jewish Forum*

Black Dog Times © 2004, *Jabberwocky Magazine*

Sonnet Against War © 2003, *Lines in the Sand, anthology*

Fat Is Not A Fairytale © 2000, *Such A Pretty Face, anthology*

"Ich Been a Yood" © 2009, *Pirene's Fountain*

St. Patrick and the Snakes © 2013, *Strange Horizons*

Fife Map © 2006, *Paradox Magazine*

Message from New Fribourgo © 2011 *Pirene's Fountain, April, Volume 4*

Dedication

For: my late cousin Honey Knopp who first taught me about politics,
    my late husband David Stemple who had
    the most amazing political rants,
    my friend Karl Finger with whom I still
    have long political conversations,
    and Jim Perlman, editor, who has helped
    me make these poems better.

Contents

I

LISTENING
TO THE NEWS

These are the turnings we were warned of,
the center imploding, the far edges
of the universe folding in upon themselves.
Now birds fall from the darkening skies;
preachers become prophets, making profits
from the end of days; a haze of obituaries;
fewer weddings and those disputed.
Notice how no celebrities look like us,
with their perfect bodies and ironed faces,
while we wrinkle like the sea.

There is no rough justice slouching
towards Bethlehem or the Arab states,
or for that matter in the courtrooms of Texas,
or the boardrooms of multinational banks.
Wall Street crumbles, the stock market stumbles,
housing starts tumble. Yeats set it all down first:
that bloody tide of change and not-change,
that bloody intensity of right and not-right,
the beast stalking the presidency
down the twisty, blackened capitol streets.
We were warned, we did not listen,
and the teeth are at the back of our necks.
Soon they will be at the front.

*"The cell phones were still ringing in the pockets of
the dead children."*
—Adam Gopnik

Not only in Aurora's movie theaters,
not only in the corridors of schools,
on the streets of Jerusalem,
Los Angeles, Chicago,
where bullet-pocked walls,
the acne of an adolescent race,
remind us how we kill with guns,
how we die, destroyed in a second,
our souls now leaden.
So generations later someone
who has traveled across the stars,
will read a poem
about the sound of cell phones
ringing in the pockets of dead children
remarking: What are cell phones?
What are guns?
What are children?

Here they come, all in a row, the children
trailing scarves of blood, slaughter
tied around their little necks.
Like a dibbuk, memory inhabits them.
Ever after, the sound of pattering rain
slamming into the thirsty ground,
will sound like the echo of gunshot.
If these children were held in the arms of angels,
they were the old ones, wings furled in flame,
faces without pity; just the awful word of God
unforgiving, without explanation,
only the promise of more to come
out of their perfect, unsullied mouths.

"(A) reminder to all of us that at times equality
can feel like a slow train coming."
—LZ Granderson

Somebody coughs.
It's cold at the station, wind blowing from the north,
blustering, posturing, blueing the children's lips.
They stamp their feet, rub mittened hands impatiently,
breathing cumulus from open mouths.
I glance down the long line.

Somebody hears
the grinding wheels on the rails right before the train
huffs into sight. We dare not grow weary, do not grow weary.
The children's laughter is the thin thread pulling the train,
like a clacketing tin toy, along the tracks, racing entropy
even as it nears.

Somebody asks,
Where is the train, where is that damned train?
A long time coming, I think, the years wear on,
and what do we have to show the children?
Only the songs, *Freedom, Freedom,*
and the dreams.

There is no trick to breathing water,
fish seem to know it, and whales,
being one with the blue, bubble jewels for eyes.
The towns surprised by the wave had no time
to teach the children to breathe before they were beneath,
no time for prayers, no time for that deep final breath.

I weep for the women whose children swam away,
whose husbands sailed off clinging to roof tops.
Mine, except for one, live safely hundreds of miles from me.
My husband died more conventionally, holding my hand.
Who can fathom the horror that wave engendered? Not I.
I can only breathe this watery air,
thankful in the moment I was not there.

—*For the mothers of Japan, 2011*

1.

1770

Confrontation invites disaster,
Don't be surprised at what comes after.

2.

Finish

After the winners,
after the also-rans,
only steel and bone,
only blood and sorrow
crosses the line.

3.

Heroes

Not just the EMTs, the policemen,
doctors, nurses, not just them,
but mothers running away with children
cradled in their arms,
an immigrant wheeling a one-legged man
to the hospital,
school children pulling smaller ones
behind them,
householders opening doors to
frightened strangers,
all, all.

4.

1770

A mob forms,
a tale worms
into history.
What follows
is no mystery.

5.

Pressure Cooker

Of a certain age, we know
that slow cookery, but this pressure
aged in the brain, comes not
to the table well seasoned,
but without reason or humanity.
In a word: insanity.

6.

Three Children Die

Whatever their ages, they are children.
Their parents scream in the night.
Dreams are of blood, dirt, the hope
of going first dashed in an instant.
Abomination is too kind a word.

7.

1770

Out of disorder, concord comes.
Out of the beating of war's fierce drums
a nation rises, flexes its might,
before we go into another dark night.

It is Autumn again
and politicians, like leaves,
stumble, tumble, fall.
The roads are scattered
with their decaying messages,
a half-life as toxic, as lasting
as uranium. Even Marie Curie
would not study these effects,
only pundits from left, right
continue to sift through the detritus,
holding the remains up,
like Incan priests lifting
the bloody hearts of victims,
reading the ruins.
It is always the same.

Every day a new hero,
who like a spike of grass
pushes through the sidewalk
ahead of the boot heel.
We do not weep .
We do not weep enough.

Faceless women
hands bound by tradition,
like the hawk in flight
turning suddenly to make
a perilous stoop.
We do not weep.
We do not weep enough.

And the children,
red flowers blossoming
on their chests,
blood of martyrs,
blood of heroes,
blood of innocents
turned knowing in that single shot.
We do not weep.
We do not weep nearly enough.

Here music is played by children on pieces of garbage
recycled, reworked, refinished, refined.
Small fingers hover over stops, strings, beating time,
though time is all they have for payment.
Music doesn't come from their fingers or mouths;
nor from strings saved from the trash,
or corroded pipes shaped into horns,
or the old canister now a drum.
It comes from the heart, that oldest dump site,
that heap of emotions, that compost of desires.

*"The Gulabi Gang is an extraordinary women's move-
ment formed in 2006 by Sampat Pal Devi in the Banda
District of Uttar Pradesh in Northern India."*
—Internet story, 2013

The *laathi* is of bamboo strong enough
to take a stripe off a man's back,
a caste mark that shouts coward,
lowering him in their fierce eyes
for what he has done to their sisters.
They have only to shake those sticks at him,
and he recants, repents, makes promises
they mean him to keep. He has seen the scars.
But more often the pink sari gang punish
with a look rather than the lash,
with shame sooner than the crack
of bamboo on skin, into fat, through bone,
bringing the hot blood after.

"Ha, ha, we won, you lost"
—Elizabeth Kerner Ewing

No wonder, then, that celebrations,
fireworks, parades, patriotic songs,
are ignored, spirit dampened
by the oceans between. Even ex-pats
find it hard to summon more than
a line of snark, a wink at the Scots.
Still on the English leash, they give back
the quiet snarl of well-trained dogs.
But what have we won, besides
a country so divided along lines
of wealth, health, and versions of God
that we cannot agree on anything,

not even our independence.

Okay, so the world didn't end today
as predicted by the preacher
who intimates that God keeps changing
His/Her unchangeable mind.
Or didn't end for me, anyway,
though a pair of Brits vacationing in Spain,
were swept away
in an accommodating flood.
A Tibetan nun set herself on fire
as the final punctuation
of a Free Tibet paragraph.
A Chinese toddler's hit-and-run death
was caught on cell phone cams
and played over more times
than the death of Gaddafi.
So maybe the preacher was right
and maybe he was wrong,
and maybe the fact that after two hours
in a restaurant where my dinner never came out.
so I left for home without eating anything,
means the world really is ending,
only one small person at a time.

How can you deny the change
when January has become
the very Florida of the year?
Thermometers perspire,
inspire walkers, who stride
across missing snowbanks,
arms bare.
                    Are you unaware
that this is no ordinary thaw?
There's a flaw in your thinking.
Mud and bud before March.
Even the daffs are threatening,
raising their green shafts
like swords, and squirrels
dig up buried nuts
in a hurry to eat
before the weather changes
its mind once again.

He is an itch, a rash that too many listeners
have to scratch, leaving a suppuration
that covers the middle of the country.
Then in a moment of madness,
he promises to move to Costa Rica
if the Supremes uphold Obamacare.
The sound you hear, that fluttering
like the wings of a million migrating birds,
are checkbooks being opened
on the East Coast, on the West,
to buy a ticket for the man.
He will go to a small country
without a standing army,
where all citizens get free health care,
a Heaven for most people
but a Hell described by Rush.

"The average uterus is 'cash only'."
—satire by Mallory Ortberg

My husband-to-be had no money when we met
which is why he had to rent rather than buy.
It made for furtive late night meetings.
fumblings in the dark, excuses and apologies.
What he gave me was fairy dollars,
looking like the real thing, but leaves in the morning.
If all love is like this to you, Mr. Politician,
I hope your wife folds up her uterus carefully
in tissue paper and talc after every use.
I know I did and it was still quite flexible
after forty-four years of marriage and a death
sealed its mouth and made it dumb again.

In my small town,
there are no levers to pull,
no chads to hang,
no touchscreens to smear
fingerprints across.
We vote the old-fashioned way,
greeting our neighbors first.
We do not ask about the vote,
but talk of weather,
the town teams,
potholes and Lyme tick.
Then pencil on paper,
heart in hand,
we mark the page.

Afterwards, I pay my land tax,
go home to drink my tea,
which is the only way
I fit a tea party into *my* voting day.

The Cossacks Are Back. May the Hills Tremble
—*New York Times,* March 2013

O, my people, memories are short,
but bones remember. And like the hills,
we tremble.

Cossacks were the reason we left our homes,
neighbors, graves of our grandparents,
braving the ocean.

They were why we left the old lives,
so our girls could work as milliners,
eyes weeping black tears.

Why our sons could drag carts behind them,
like cattle, sweating patches dark as blood
under their arms.

O, my people, revenge has a long lash
and the skin remembers.
But unlike the hills, we do not remain.

The headlines shout even louder
than the people in the streets,
as if to convince us of tragedy.
We are so surfeited with horror,
yet another zombie mash-up,
feeding on the blood and bones
of bad news, we cannot bother
to close our door, double bolt it
against another bomb or drone.
Terrorism has become a video game,
mothers' tears, something to bottle up
and sell on QVC along with ginzu knives,
cheap jewelry, brand knock-offs.
I know I should watch, but change
the channel, searching instead
for Castle re-runs, where bad guys
get put away in an hour, tops,
instead of a seven-year search,
long past the time of my caring.
When did I pack my heart away,
cold case my soul? I still hear myself
at age sixteen weeping in the cupboard
under the stairs. Perhaps I should leave
a plate of fresh baked chocolate chip cookies
by the door, for that small shadow,
who still believes in a just world.

"Where one burns books, one will eventually burn people."
—Heinrich Heine

Long before Bradbury warned us,
we knew that burning books
could consume us all.
I had a book torched once,
a conflagration on the steps
of the K.C. Board of Education.
Taken from the library, my book
was set on a hibachi, match lit.

My words browned and writhed on the page,
sentences screamed, paragraphs begged for life.
Before the arson could be stopped,
a year of my writing went up in flames.
Far away on the East Coast of America
I felt the heat of it burning my cheeks.

Somewhere in Germany, an old man dances.

"It's late but everything comes next."
—Naomi Shihab Nye

That clock stands at five to midnight,
or if you shift your head slightly,
five to noon. Your choice.
These things are always a choice.
We do not have to build more barriers.
They will unbuild themselves in time,
The world is like that if we let it
Un-sew, unknit, loosen the bonds.
I like to think of us walking backwards,
finding a vineyard, sitting on the ground,
eating dates, drinking the sweet water
gushing from the desert, making flowers grow.
I do not throw stones. You shall not eat them.
Shalom Aleichem I say softly to you.
You respond, *Aleichem shalom.*
It is the start of everything.

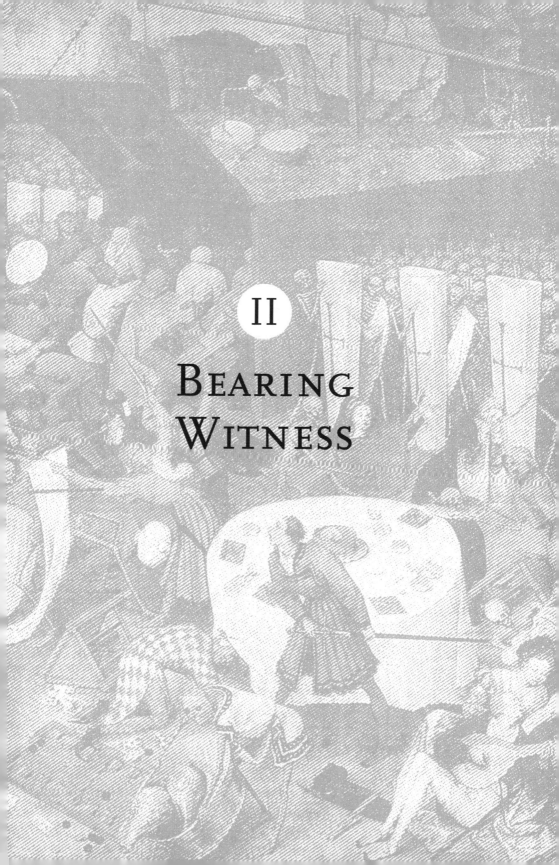

II

BEARING
WITNESS

ARC

"<The> arc of the moral universe is long,
but it bends toward justice."
—Theodore Parker

Teeter-tottering in the universe,
riding humanity's carousel,
drawing lines in the sandbox,
all those references to childhood
when it is past time for us to grow up.
How easily we forget those darker siblings
hungering for their own fair play
on the far side of the fence.
Haven't we discussed this before?
Haven't we found ourselves wanting--
or is it just wanting more?
Such questions do not get to the center.
As we go up and down, antic calliope
drowning out the rising cries for help,
am I the only one thinking:
the arc isn't going to bend itself?

It is your fault, says the gun,
I have no argument with the dead.
I am metal and air, smoke and fire,
I worship the maker, have no other truth.

It is your fault, says the bullet,
I have no argument with the fallen,
I ask no questions, go where I'm sent,
I worship the barrel, have no other truth.

It is your fault, says the seller,
I have no argument with the target,
I seek that I might find, sell that I might live,
I worship the dollar, have no other truth.

It is your fault, says the shooter,
I have no argument with the victims,
I am all bleak thoughts, hard words,
I worship the darkness, have no other truth.

Then it is my fault, says the child,
Blood singing from her wounds,
Innocence leaking from her eyes,
I worship the future, have no other...

NEWS

There is no good news
that is not bad news
to someone else,
Every messiah rises
from the bloody bodies
of the people above, below.
The Jews know this best,
the gypsies, the blacks,
Sacrifices continue,
a lash to the back,
a slash to the throat,
the corn god dead, arisen.
We hang from the nail
drink the bug juice,
are hanged, drawn, quartered, skinned,
then die for someone else's sins.

True minds, two minds,
to minds married
there is no impediment.
(Latin—*impedire*, to ensnare.)
But have we got it wrong
all this time?
What is finer than to be
tangled in love's snares,
to be taken unawares
by long looks, dark hairs.
To climb the tower stairs
and see Rapunzel with the witch
breast to breast on the bed,
love to love,
tongue to tongue,
head to head.

True minds, two minds,
mind you, without impediment
become this day married.
(Latin—*maritus*, husband.)
But have we got it wrong
all this time?
What is truer than two,
coming in the ark,
coming in the dark,
and through till morning's single lark
sings lustily from the park
to waken Cinderella from

her sister's bed,
breast to breast,
love to love,
tongue to tongue.
head to head.

—*For Delia and Ellen*

"'I have the kiss of Walt Whitman still on my lips,' he boasted."
— Neil McKenna, *Secret Life of Oscar Wilde*

So big deal, two poets kiss,
touch knees, have sex.
Furtive in their movements
or boldly on a table in a restaurant,
scaring the horses or the patrons
or a certain pursed-lipped lady,
second booth to the left.
News at eleven.

When will this be no more
than a squib, a squiggle,
a gossip column item?
The firmament doesn't shift,
God doesn't fall precipitously
from an alabaster throne,
nations do not rise or founder
because Oscar and Walt got it on,
because Oscar boasted
and Walt didn't deny.

I have considered the Rapture
and found it wanting,
promising a heaven
of such narrow-mindedness,
without character, humor,
caring or compassion
that I can only guess it's a devil's ploy.

What kind of God demands a mother
take boxcutters to her daughters' throats.
What kind of paradise is worth losing
the friends who fed my family and me
through the dark days of my husband's death?
What eternity is worth the slaughter
of millions of innocents across a globe?

That is tyranny, not religion,
Do not do this in the name of my God
or your God or our lack of belief in any God.
Surely there is a place for the good,
whatever or whoever they believe in
whether he has a beard, she has breasts,
they have tentacles, or *d.* none of the above.

How can I tell you this? How can I not?
There is a word that fills my mouth,
that makes me smile and understand the world
for maybe the first time ever.
Traghairm.
It means to prophesy
while wrapped in a bullock's skin
behind a waterfall,
an entire story, a culture, a magic, a happening
in a single word

How can I tell you this? How can I not?
See him, this seer, naked except for that skin,
shivering in the spray, praying, throwing the bones,
picking through entrails, entranced,
hair slicked down with dreams.
When he emerges, what will he tell us?
That the world is ending, beginning,
concentrating, flying apart?
That there will be bank failures,
suicides, brown grass, ozone ruptures?
That the great blue glaciers and the great blue whales,
equal survivors of ages, are doomed?
That owls and frogs and white tigers and salamanders
best be caught in our lenses before they are gone?

He can see it all, without a tv, without reading the *Sunday Times,*
without consulting the *Farmer's Almanac*
or his neighbor's copy of *Edgar Cayce* or the *Book of the Dead.*
All he needs is a bullock's skin and a waterfall.
All he needs is a word,
like *inauguration.*

I am told there is grass at Auschwitz
And people picnic there again
Beside the iron maw that swallowed
The expended children. Good wine,
White from the Rhineland, flows
From open necks down laughing mouths.
And papers litter the ominous mounds,
Receptacles that cry for truth.

If we forget these, will our tongues
Cleave to dry mouths or hands
Hang helpless at our sides? Unstrung
The harps of this new exile
Whisper from the swaying trees:
This exile soft, this new God quick
To ease our memories.

It is with humanity more fine we choose
To hum the dead alive with laughter
Than wail the grave, and martyred Jews?

I was not in Boston that day,
but close enough,
the borders of our state porous.

Horror slipped through from the South.
We had already wept with the children,
the teachers of Newtown.

But we go unarmed into the future.
The tea we left as undrinkable
three centuries ago we will not drink now.

Still, what of this legless terror
leeching through Commonwealth soil,
reaching my house ninety miles west?

I cannot put up fences. Our poet laureate
of New England told us
they make good neighbors.

But lousy friends, we add,
keeping our doors open
to our town kin and terror alike.

I've been thinking about democracies,
Theocracies, bureaucracies, hypocrisies.
Been thinking about totalities, moralities,
Fatalities, and ballotries.
Been thinking about the vote.

Been thinking about succeeding, seceding,
Proceeding, conceding,
And about the aging of America
Plus my own crow feet.

Been thinking about veins and vanity,
About my neighbor Maddow, and Hannity.
Been thinking about pundits and punning,
And pruning, and grooming, and running away.
Been thinking about the vote.

Been thinking about you and me,
About chains and being free,
About democracy and O Say Can You See.
      Been thinking about,
      Been thinking about,
      Been thinking about the vote.

Explain it to me, this passion for the cruel,
fifty shades of pain, I don't get it.
For me, pain is a wakeup call from disease,
or whispers from a rose thorn
buried deep in the thumb,
an aside from a toe numb
from too much stumbling,
shout from a hip banged
against a table edge,
throat clear from an esophagus
already rough from a night's coughing.

To be cruel wastes pain.
It plants only fear, prunes only anger,
composts only fury,
waits for the bitter harvest.

"Thomas More used to say, it's like sporting with a tamed lion. You tousle its mane and pull its ears, but all the time you're thinking, those claws, those claws, those claws."
—Hilary Mantel, from *Bring Up the Bodies*

There is always a time when the kings have claws,
sharp, dirty, reddened, grim;
times when the people have them.
I am not sure what time we have left.
I should take box cutters, scissors,
or a good honest knife for the work,
but I cannot stand the cries of pain.
Whoever said that the tree of liberty
must be watered by the blood of martyrs
did not see the Towers go down
or the jumpers floating the first hundred floors
like angels, wingless on their way to earth.
Did not see the first president I ever voted for
slump against his wife's pink suit
in a car speeding quickly towards heaven.
The lion does not care who he injures, kills,
only likes the smell of blood, the sound of crunching.
Kings, presidents, dictators, too,
never learn the names of the dead, the dying,
the families casually raked with their claws.
When *we* kill, the names are lost as well.
Who are the martyrs then? Who the lions?

We all whisper morse, the coding that binds,
an IRA handshake, Yiddish for the Jew,
Mandarin amongst the Chinese, the talk of thread that winds
through the milliner's trade, Sioux with Sioux.
The deaf with coded fingers gossip with their own.
Puffs of smoke, drums, hieroglyphs, holy writ.
Everyone sings to the choir, crown to crown.
We morse in blood, in semen, in sweat, in spit.

There is no group that speaks for the world.
We signal with secret words, hand-held signs,
with semaphores, banners, flags unfurled
along the vigil and striker lines.
And we women course through tidal weeks,
comparing labor pains, of which no man speaks.

The world will end when the old woman finishes her porcupine quill
blanket, though her black dog unpicks it whenever her back is turned
—Lakota legend

What can you do in these black dog times?
When the world is close to done,
And only the dog's teeth stand between us
And the ending? What can you do?
Choose to be born, stand up, pick the quills,
See through the mist, through the dark.
Sew yourself a robe, not a shroud.
Age gracefully. Take your medicine.
Have a colonscopy. Do not complain.
Pick up your skirts, bend your aching knees,
And dance.

III

POEMS NEVER
TURN AWAY

"(T)he language women speak when there's
no one around to correct them."
—Hélène Cixous

We speak to oranges first thing in the morning,
the slow peel, the soft crunch, juices awakening
night's palate, the spurt of acid on the chin.

We speak to coffee, to tea, telling it how sleep
is for the weak, the lonely, for men who collapse
at the first pillow touch, for children whose play
has exhausted them, for others not us.

We speak to the chorus of birds outside, as awake,
as alive as we are in the every dawn, as alert
to the nuance of cloud, of wind, of breath.

We speak to the flowers in our gardens, the real ones
and the ones we nurture in our hearts.
Not just careful tulips, daffodils in rows,
but the wild eruptions of poppies, rosebay willow-herb
cultivated by bird, bee, breeze, and brush in the disturbed spaces.

We speak to the walkway that calls to the horizon,
the horizon that signals to the imprisoned heart.
This is how we speak when there is no one around
to scold, to correct, to tell us how we must speak.

I am a woman, I hold the child
Under the breastbone, close to the heart;
I wash the linens, crusty and soiled,
I pile dead bodies on to the cart.
I am a woman, I feed the soldiers,
Hungry and hopeless, milk from my breast;
I rock the cradles, I move the boulders,
I am a woman, I get no rest.

I am a woman, I am the witness,
I cry to heaven; if I'm not heard,
I write the pamphlets, I make the impress,
I am the woman, I know the word.
Better be careful, men who make war,
We woman know what we're fighting for.

And this is no country for old women.
The internet chats, the movies, songs,
all sing of youth and time. Forgotten,
challenged by gravity, by memory, we long
for the past, though it is long past time when
we can recall the splendors that once rang
through us like Old Tom's mighty knell.
We are in some strange notion of Hell.

How did we get here? Step by step
along the unforgiving path of time.
How do we leave here? Stop by stop,
along the train's slip line, become
childish, childlike, inelegant, inept,
back to the beginning, back to the womb,
to the heartbeat, the blood beat in the ear
that only the fetus and the women can hear.

"...you'd come to class and find a note tacked to the door:
Grace is in jail".
—Dani Shapiro on Grace Paley as her writing
    teacher, in an interview in *Salon*

My first thought on finding the note
was that Grace, along with Mercy
had been arrested in a vigil
that had, as usual, gotten out of hand.
Grace was the one striking poses,
giving the pigs the finger,
looking beautiful, all the paparazzi,
focusing on her as if she was
the people's princess instead of
a nice Jewish girl from the Bronx.

And Mercy, bless her heart,
a good southern girl from Charleston,
always interceding for those in need,
and those who did not, saying *sir*
to the cop as she climbed on his back,
beating him soundly with her perfectly
formed small fists and the pearly nails,
newly polished that morning.

They were probably accompanied by
Sloth and Insolence, the latter
not named in any Biblical exegesis,
so could come and go at will,
making cutting remarks as if he had
a knife actually in his hand.

No one noticed him, of course,
his attendance only hearsay.

But Sloth, once again lay down
before the barricades ready
to trip the police, and was lifted
onto the tumbrel and slumbered
all the way to jail but hailed
by the brothers since he'd gone
along with Mercy and Grace, because--
as the newspaper wits wrote in four columns,
Grace is who you get but don't deserve,
Mercy who you don't get, even if you *do* deserve.
And Sloth, well he just comes with the package.

*"...they simply do not believe in anything fervently
enough to go to jail for it."*
—Maxine Kumin

For liberty, which seems an oxymoron.
For free speech, when I want to be paid for it.
For nuclear protests, though I wish for power.
For anti-war sentiments though I could have killed Nazis,
 heroin purveyors, child slavers, serial rapists,
 murderers, paedophiles without looking back.
But my fervor is saved for family and storytelling.
Enough to stay out of jail for,
 And I am fervent about that.

I am thinking of a fairy tale,
Cinder Elephant,
Sleeping Tubby,
Snow Weight,
where the princess is not
anorexic, wasp-waisted,
flinging herself down the stairs.

I am thinking of a fairy tale,
Hansel and Great
Repoundsel,
Bounty and the Beast,
where the beauty
has a pillowed breast,
and fingers plump as sausage.

I am thinking of a fairy tale
that is not yet written,
for a teller not yet born,
for a listener not yet conceived,
for a world not yet won,
where everything round is good:
the sun, wheels, cookies, and the princess.

We sit at home and watch the news,
Our conscience caught upon the screen:
Black against white, Muslims, Jews.
We push the mute to damp the scene.

We send a check off for the cause
And feel a savior, right and clean.
And then, without a moment's pause,
We change the channel on the screen.

> Too late my friends for turning back,
> I am what I am, you are what you are,
> Overhead the sky goes black.
> We all must wear the yellow star.

We hear the sound of breaking glass,
Ground under boot heel, very fine.
Life is taken though it should pass,
And you have grabbed up what was mine.

Once again the wind is sighing,
One again the words come hard,
Once again the young are dying
Under the eyes of a sullen guard.

> Too late my friends for turning back,
> I am what I am, you are what you are.
> Overhead the sky goes black.
> We all must wear the yellow star,

We are what we are, the ape made man.
We wield the stick as tool, as gun.
We do what we do and not what we can
And heaven help us if we run.

The signs have come and they have gone,
Like gods they suddenly appear.
The signs are burning on the lawn
And I am old enough to care.

Too late my friends for turning back.
I am what I am, you are what you are,
Overhead the sky goes black.
We all must wear the yellow star.

After reading a Holocaust anecdote in Barbara
Rush's "Book of Jewish Women's Tales"

The rabbi's daughter,
savaged by a thousand cuts,
a thousand bites
from Grayze's dogs,
called out for each cut, each bite
that she was a Jew and would not kneel.
She died, on her knees,
but not kneeling
for she stood upright at the throne of God.
God, I wish I had such courage
to not-kneel in the face of outrage,
the teeth of tyranny,
the knives of the unholy.
Instead I change the channels,
I turn the page,
I write a small poem
in the rabbi's daughter's honor,
I, who do not even know her name.

Driving them out of Ireland,
his hand on the wheel,
the smallest of the snakes asking,
"Are we there yet?"
Patrick wonders if it is a good idea.
It had seemed so at the time,
all those snakes among the green
demeaning the glory.
It had made him sick, those fellows
in the grass, narrow, startling.
Still, didn't even the meanest creatures
the belly crawlers, the finaglers,
the seducers of Eden, deserve a home?
Who is he to claim Ireland only for himself?

He tells them to shut their cake holes,
stop hissing and pissing about the ride.
He needs to think about Christ,
figure out what the Holy Spirit wants.
His fingers on the wheel turn white
as he yanks it hard, heads for home
hoping he will not regret it,
asking himself: *What would Jesus do?*

WWJD

What would Jesus do
if he came back today?
Work the soup kitchens,
greet the immigrants,
march against big banks,
teach ESL.
He would be called a socialist,
a communist,
a Muslim,
a Jew,
an illegal alien,
a hippie,
an agitator,
faggot,
geek.
He would be deported,
or lynched,
or tied to the bumper of a car
and dragged to his death,
you know, the same old same old,
while we, the howling mob,
catch it on our cells,
upload it to YouTube,
and he would go viral
just like last time,
another word for Heaven
and fifteen minutes of fame.

1.

Goosey, goosey gander,
What an open-hander,
Running for the senate
Gathering the plunder.
Will he win November?
I will take that bet.
He has raised the most dough
In the race yet.

2.

Mister Merry,
Quite contrary,
How does your country grow?
This country's built
With silver gilt
And immigrants all in a row.

3.

What a Boehner,
What a groaner.
What a massive pit.
We sit in this puddle
Up to our middle
And can't get out of it.

4.

Humpledy Dumpledy,
Tossed from a wall;
Employment soon followed
This terrible fall.
All of the army
And all the reserves,
Got to give Humpeldy
What he deserves.

5.

Ring around the senate,
To fly Tea Party pennant.
They're asses, they're asses.
We *all* fall down.

"The beggars have changed places but the lash goes on..."
—W.B. Yeats

Reading the news is like bending
under the lash of history.
I feel the welts rise up,
but cannot see them,
even when I turn my head.
Fox News nips at our heels,
its teeth shining with drawn blood.
We ignore it, running down the long path,
carrying our brothers, our sisters,
the least of these, on our backs,
upon our shoulders, in our arms.
A nip is just one more small wound.
A person could die from such fine cuts.

Where do we go from here,
having already torn this world into pieces?
Some say we go into the next.
But ploughshare in hand, I say
we only have this now, this here, this earth,
as I set down my burdens,
learn their old wisdoms,
teach them to plant another seed.

"A well regulated Militia, being necessary to the security of a free State..."
—U.S. Constitution

So you want your guns,
you sons
of security,
the purity
of longing,
and belonging
to the state.
So you want your sons
well armed
and furthermore
well armored.
And your daughters too,
when she's out
on a date.
Every floozy
with an ouzi,
every mom
with a bomb,
every usher
in a rush
to cover customers
in seats.
Rocket launchers
for the lunchers,
who are eating out in towns.
And we'll buy guns
for the pious
who can hide them
in their gowns.

So you need
an armed militia,
every Patrick
and Patricia,
so-called Patriots
patrolling
making mean streets
really mean.
And the only ones
who benefit
supplying
all these
armies
are the ones who make
their living
(and our dying)
really
green.

Yes, he knows the questions,
but he does not know the answers.
His brain knocks, nudges, puzzles,
does not let him sleep at night.
Not knowing is a pebble in the shoe,
that never ceases to annoy
even when the sock is stripped away.
Whatever answers I give him
are not enough. He does not trust them.
He is mad with the dark pathways
that I dance down so easily,
If he is cruel with me,
he is crueler with himself.
I forgive him in the end.
I know where I am going,
the answers in my pocket,
the fork ahead a treasure.
It is all about the road.

I would embrace change gladly
if the damned thing would stand still
long enough for me to wrap my arms
around its eely body. If its snaky locks
would stop giving me the Medusa stare.
If it did not smell like death, like an old boot,
like Brussel sprouts in the overnight pan.
If its touch wasn't ice, shards in my heart,
when I am looking for a dram of warm comfort.
Oh, I would embrace change, if it didn't mean
you dying, the children growing up and away,
girlfriends talking behind my back,
editors moving west or starting a boutique,
friends marrying the wrong women,
that kind of change.
I'm looking to embrace upward mobility,
saving the whales, a chance at a big grant,
banning fracking, delivering the death blow
to the Tea Party, a smart funny man in my bed.
Though not you. Never you again. Even I
know an un-embraceable fantasy when I write it.

These Scottish names, no longer
markers of the king's passage:
High Place of Pigs, Fort by the River,
Church Headland, Browed Hill.
We think we read all of history
in the lines of a map,
our rough mangling of names
but one more imperialism.
Still the land, now broken
apart, cut, scythed, slit,
plowed, lumbered, flattened,
mounded, diverted, cauterized,
shamed by iron and steel,
will outlast our poor map
with its thin bloodlines of roads.
Fife will one day be eaten by grass,
its names erased,
the headstones blank boulders
written on by rain, by river,
by the long passage of time,
till we become but fossils
telling the new past to the new future
who will read the names
of their new kingdom
by the light of familiar stars.

"China to Flatten 700 Mountains to Build A City"
—Time Magazine

There it is, the key to human problem-solving
a fortune cookie plan found in the Bible, I'm sure:
flatten mountains, drown planets, retrofit landscapes,
part great rivers, destroy populations, move mighty armies.
Never mind the part about loaves, fishes, rainbows,
rams in the brambles, raising the dead, the fall of sparrows.
Don't think about neighbors and the meek inheritance.
Them roads gotta roll.
We R Armageddon.
There's deals to be done,
money to be made.
A parade to organize.
Cities to rise.
And more.
Hear us roar.

News is carried so swiftly these days,
we have more unsettled time to worry.
I read of mudslides, raging rivers
in my brother's region of Brazil,
where folks have built too swiftly
on the lush green hillsides,
mindful neither of swelling rivers,
nor the land sliding into houses.
As quickly as the news flashes,
like lightning over Nova Friburgo,
the email comes, and skype after.
Six hundred neighbors missing, dead.

But my brother and his family are safe.
Their dogs conscious of the sound of mud,
still shudder their animal fears,
little runneling worms under the skin.
Half my nephew's garden is gone,
his red and gold flowers, like Persephone,
buried underground far from the sun.
We do not dance our joy, or sing it out,
but like school boarders
raiding the dormitory kitchen,
we quickly stuff our mouths
with sweets and swallow
before we are found out and punished
with a cane, a demerit, more mud.

PAINTING ANGELS

"For every locomotive they build, I shall paint another angel."
—Edward Burne-Jones

For every bomb, every frack,
every drill that pierces the planet's heart,
for every spew of auto carbons,
every stealth plane mounting the sky,
for every bit of asbestos hiding in an attic,
every coal mine scarring a mountain,
I shall write a poem.

For every child dying in a war zone,
every infant left on a doorstep,
every child raped in the nighttime,
or kept in a cupboard, a valise, a small room,
for every child who wakes frightened,
who sleeps unfed, uncared for,
I shall write a poem.

In this world there is no end of weeping,
no end of sorrow, no end of pain,
and now there will be no end of poems.

When life is a blevit of failure and grief
We carry on carrying on.
When life is so tres, even nothing's relief,
We carry on carrying on.

When things of the future are things of the past,
When death is before us and first is the last,
When everything comes as a TNT blast,
We carry on carrying on.

When all the mananas are dwindling down,
When slips on bananas are tattered and brown,
When it's too hard to smile and much simpler to frown,
We carry on carrying on.

I'll carry on you, if you'll carry on me
On a tres filled with sorrow, and crackers and brie.
And the only thing tres-er is so tres jollie
That we carry on carrying on.

"Poems, though, never turn away... they wait patiently."
—Rachel Hadas

Like priests, like undertakers, like soldiers, like spies,
poems never turn away, never shrug from us,
never look at the floor, check their watches furtively.
Even if we forget poems, the pages of their books grown dusty,
the broadsides crumpled, crumbled, foxed, forgotten,
they wait to give us counsel, courage, content in their lines.
Anonymous in black robes, uniforms,
the epaulettes of sorrow on their shoulders,
black and red medals of love clanking on their chests,
poems linger unceasing in boardrooms, bedrooms,
in common rooms, bathrooms, throne rooms,
and in the chambers of our shrunken hearts,
waiting with patience till they can speak.

About the Author

Jane Yolen, often called "the Hans Christian Andersen of America," is the author of over 340 books, including *Owl Moon, The Devil's Arithmatic* and *How Do Dinosaurs Say Goodnight.* The books range from rhymed picture books and baby board books, through middle grade fiction, poetry collections, nonfiction, and up to novels and story collections for young adults and adults, and eight books of adult poetry.

Her books and stories have won an assortment of awards—two Nebulas, a World Fantasy Award, a Caldecott, the Golden Kite Award, three Mythopoetic awards, two Christopher Medals, a nomination for the National Book Award, and the Jewish Book Award, among others. She is also the winner (for body of work) of the Kerlan Award, the World Fantasy Assn. Lifetime Achievement Award, and the Catholic Library's Regina Medal. Six colleges and universities have given her honorary doctorates.

Visit her website at: *www.janeyolen.com*